Spinning the Stone

poems by

Jana Bouma

Finishing Line Press
Georgetown, Kentucky

Spinning the Stone

For Brad and Chandra

Copyright © 2025 by Jana Bouma
ISBN 979-8-89990-049-5 First Edition
All rights reserved under International and Pan-American Copyright Conventions. No part of this book may be reproduced in any manner whatsoever without written permission from the publisher, except in the case of brief quotations embodied in critical articles and reviews.

Publisher: Leah Huete de Maines
Editor: Christen Kincaid
Cover Art and Design: Deborah Goschy
Author Photo: Steve Pottenger

Order online: www.finishinglinepress.com
also available on amazon.com

Author inquiries and mail orders:
Finishing Line Press
PO Box 1626
Georgetown, Kentucky 40324
USA

Contents

Paying Attention 1

I. The Body Remembers
Back to the Earth 5
Incipience 6
First Light 7
The Body Remembers 8
What can I have to say, child, ... 9
Swimming Dock, Longville, Minnesota 10
What if each of us 11
Solid Things 12
Visiting My Father 13
December Morning 14
The One Thing 15
Afternoon Call 16
Song of the Seventh Day 17

Section II. Maladies
Color Shift 21
Causing a Stir 22
In Which He Tries to Make Me Understand 23
The Things We Forget 24
In the Open 26
What I Did That Day 27
The Knife 28
Standing Upright 29
Fleeing Nebraska 30
Transcontinental 31

Dead Metaphors 32
Institutional Memory.. 33
Embrace 35
Landscape with Trees 36
Updraft.. 37
You are a teenage girl 38
Raising the Temperature.. 40

Section III. The Earth's Skin
Spinning the Stone 43
Earth's Bones 44
Forty-seven Miles above Lock Number 1 45
Stripes.. 47
The Poet Is Asked to Write about a Tree 48
Paddling the Mississippi, South of St. Cloud............................. 49
Sunday Morning Samba 50
The cold of January.. 51
Hearing the News 52
First of June 54
Two Visits to Paradise 55
The Famous Anoka Potato 56
January Morning, Lake Superior, Rocky Beach......................... 57
Beside the Kennedy Expressway 58
Terror wore us... 59

Acknowledgments.. 60

*We love the earth we came from, and the sky
we're lofted into, and (first and last) words.*
—Connie Wanek

Paying Attention

after a photograph, "Bucket," by Danny Mansk

Sometimes a light shines
from deep within a thing.
A thing worn, well-used.
An old shoe, a wooden stool,
a rusted sign hanging above the door.
Sometimes the light spills, buttermilk-yellow,
and you don't have to do a thing to feel
refreshed as if drinking from a cool pail.
Sometimes it shines from an old face
passing on the sidewalk.
It will carry you, in a dream, to a familiar street
where you walk, shaded by the trees
that you know are no longer there.

I
The Body Remembers

Back to the Earth

after a painting by Rachel Orman

how quickly we forget
the watery chaos
the primordial
reds and yellows
the sinews taking liquid
shape the heat expanding
toward form breast
      hip
jealousy
           ovum
   anger
 fingertip
a sudden emptying
an embodied self
drawn forth
ruddy
still hot

Incipience

Even more than the silent end of the month
I recognize the signs the ache in the breasts
the sudden fatigue my hands feeling distant
on the steering wheel we have waited so long
for me to need that first appointment the sound
of the heartbeat I give you the news you smile
your usual effusive self your arms around me
briefly now I sit unable to move
my life so light so pliable so
inconsequent ending beginning another
an unknown gift a weight a dark and yawning
courtyard a hero's journey a long slow binding
another life beginning what
life
what
life

First Light

You will remember your first glimpse of me,
the clenched fists, arms and legs outflung,

the skin glistening, slick and streaked with blood,
the strident, implacable wail, cry of severance.

The moment the rooting mouth finds it place
and the two of us are brought forth, together,
into wide-eyed silence.

The Body Remembers

Again the cry, the bleating, hiccupping, insect buzz.
The world come to this: Covers thrown back, body rising,

feet shuffling their worn path across the hall, past the streetlamp's
bars and shadows. Bending to see the red face, the balled fists,

the arms and knees pulled to the chest, quivering. Lifting
the small heaviness, feeling the rounded firmness of bones,

muscle, and flesh, the tender rolls on forearm and thigh,
the hardness of down-covered skull. Brushed by that small, open blossom,

tilting, rooting, resistless, the breast gives the familiar response,
the tingle, the spreading warmth, the rush of the milk, ready, eager.

Once more, the kneading fist, the slow-sweeping, feathered eyelids,
the satisfied, inexorable rhythm, the world a place of milky, sweetsour
darkness.

What can I have to say, child,

about the chocolate smears beside the mouth,
the cheeks as round as apples,
the fingers grasping the fat handle
while the eyes gaze from the photo
with a Sufi mystic's intensity?
The hand guides the toothbrush
(already the dutiful rituals), but there is no pause
in the eager interrogation—
the smooth, the pebbled, the sharp, the pliant, the heavy,
the sweet, the pungent—
this indefatigable calling forth of a young
and reciprocal world.

Swimming Dock, Longville, MN

The four of them propel the little boat from the beach
to the wooden platform, where they tie off

and scramble up, adjust their bathing suits, giggle and jostle,
feint and half-step toward the water. They stand here

because they do not want to face the shoreline's gentle slope,
the step and hesitation, the recoil of timid flesh at the water's icy rise.

No. Here above these clear depths, they may pause for one
moment's anticipation, a season of glances. Then,

a thunder of feet, a chorus of shrieks, and their bodies
take flight, arms pointed prayerfully, legs akimbo, soaring toward

that spasm of chill surprise by which they're baptized,
feeling their bodies open, saying, *Yes, yes.*

What if each of us

were a window what
if wherever we moved
the mountains shone
through us
or the dark, curling wave or
the childhood home that we'd
forgotten
tattered shingles, hollyhocks upright
like soldiers
beside the high white door

what if reaching
out to touch you I felt
the meadow's heart
beating
the earth's granite carapace
what if leaning
close I heard the ocean's salt roar

let us stand, the four
of us, side by side
they will look at us and see
the sweeping arc across the black void
the blue, glowing rim of this our delicate

planet

Solid Things

I dreamt a concrete wall
that took itself apart,
each heavy rectangle
lifting, settling, blocks
jumping other blocks,
high-stepping down the road,
clouds of birds rising,
alarmed, from the trees.

I wondered why
a wall decided
to no longer be a wall,
and whether my own
parts would decide
to take themselves apart
one day, toes and
ears, fingers and
cells dispersing
and disappearing
into the deep blue
distances.

Visiting My Father

each of his days
was a glimpse
through a
high window
of some
cloud-obscured
planet small
against the
blackness each
day was a snail's
shell transparent
and empty
each day was
the silence
of a horse
galloping in
the distance a
telegraph
receiver at which
he listened for
the click
of a message
from someone
who had forgotten
his name

December Morning

Fierce wind. Along the trail,
echinacea cones rattle.
The delicate crowns of the trees
overflow with emptiness.

The One Thing

Consider the trachea,
passageway of muscle fiber,
unity dividing itself into
left and right bronchi,
the smaller bronchioles,
the alveoli, clustered chambers
trussed in nets of blood. Consider
the smooth and glistening tissue,
fissured and lobed, the semilunar base,
mediastinal impression deepening
around the heart.

Consider the chest's rise and fall,
the coolness in the nasal passages,
the downward plunge of the diaphragm,
intermingling of inner and outer
across the permeable curtain.

Consider the rhythmic pant of the runner,
the sleeper's quiet exhale,
the diva's high C, vibrating,
the lover's gasp and sigh.
The mother watches the sleeping infant,
the child's breathing quick and shallow.
A pause—the mother waiting, waiting
for, ah, the next breath.

And the end. Smoke-blackened.
Or, the steady, dependable cycle until
the bullet, or the clot.
A forgetful, open-mouthed slowing
while the cheeks hollow, the eyes stare,
the companion waits beside the bed
for the final sigh.

Afternoon Call

a haibun

"The phone keeps cutting out," I tell him. "What did you say?" It's not the phone, my brother replies, it's the tumors compressing his trachea. Last week's x-ray showed one tumor; today's scan shows them in the lymph nodes, the liver, the bones. I don't know whether his tears are for himself, his wife, or his child.

Robin feeds her young.
One side of the lilac tree blossoms,
one stands bare.

Song of the Seventh Day

I miss your hands.
Hold them close to the camera so I can kiss them.
Let them graze the edge of my thoughts like a whisker.
Let them take hold of my door knob heart,
pry up the shingles until I'm open to the sky.

Your hands are two sparrows rising and settling,
one melody playing in two different keys.

Let your hands dance with the knives of memory's kitchen.
Let them turn up time's collar and unpack midnight's duffel bag.
Let them find the small wounds.
Let them fold up my memories like a suitcase.

Without your hands, the windows weep,
the laundry unfolds itself, the lamps forget to burn.

Send me your hands; my dreams will clap wildly, the leaves will fly upward.
Send me your hands; let them bring me my breakfast, pour me my wine.
Send me your hands of rhinestone and buttermilk, night sky and roses.
I miss your heart-singing, dawn-enfolding, longing-born hands.

II
Maladies

Color Shift

Put away the pictures. That's what you get
after thirty-seven years—a goddamn Kool-Aid-stained world,
every one of us glowing with a cherry sunburn,
like rosy cherubs or fire-faced Sunday drunks. Bad enough
those fools at the reception, smiling like it's a blessed day, like
they're watching the bride and groom march off
into happily-after-ever, like we don't all know
what really happened (how quick the acid ate through that veil).

Even worse—that shit-eating grin
on the face of Mr. Most-Likely-to-Succeed,
sliding into his blue blaze-of-glory tuxedo.
We know where he's headed—toward
that drunken poker game that'll cost him the family business,
toward 2 a.m. on a Tuesday morning,
the last time his son will slam the door in his face,
toward fifteen years of mumbling from the couch
every time his daughter and son-in-law come to visit.
(She was a sweet girl, not that he'd have noticed.)

And what about Margie, there in the background?
Slender. Black hair sleek as the coat of a young filly.
There she is, and she doesn't guess—
no one guesses—where she'll be by Christmas. Even before then,
she'll have lost it all—the hair, the perfect skin,
the pieces they carved away to try and stop it.
They did have the wedding, Tommy standing by her hospital bed,
the bride's father bowed over his fists on the far side of the room.
Yeah, look at her beautiful smile.

As for the rest of us—don't ask. Who wants to hear
about the divorces, the pot bellies and bad teeth,
the friends turned into sons-of-bitches, the women collapsed into themselves,
the young men who won't be coming back from the war.
Yeah, we got pictures. We got pictures of all of them.

Causing a Stir

Descending on the town, snakes and dragons purpling their skin,
bike engines roaring – Yes, ma'am, the two of them
caused quite a stir.

They finger the pebbled path in darkness, these garden revenants.
Midnight heliotrope, brittle spiderwort,
death-white aster.

She drags it across cold marble, this slow-yielding weight, this clotted
heaviness. It has to do with you, what you might
ask of her.

A night without a moon. You'll take the county road toward town,
expect the storefronts' empty silences. Main Street throbs with light.
All the town's astir.

She left a note and a rabbit's foot. She dragged his Harley
from the shed, kicked it til it roared,
and went on a wild-ass tear.

In Which He Tries to Make Me Understand

The way you run after a child in traffic. The way you pick at a scab that threatens to heal. The way butter melts on a slice of toast. The way an excavator peels back earth. The way the orange rind shrivels to dullness on a granite countertop. The way, at the beach, your dog's body turns and drops to meet fish skeleton. The way your wife looks different to you the next morning, for no reason in particular. The way the moth unrolls its proboscis into the well of the flower. The way the car uncrumples as the clock runs backwards. The way the knife finds the notch between rib and rib. Scarlet. The way a fourteen-year-old boy looks at a stranger who's asked him a question. The way socks lie, emptied, at the end of the day. The way you hold your lover's arm and touch where the cancer used to be. The way the father sits but does not speak to his son holding the phone behind the glass.

The Things We Forget

My dentist warns that my gums are letting go—
threatening to set my teeth adrift on a current of words.
So I bought myself an electric toothbrush,
and my teeth, now, after brushing them
are so clean that they are a wonder,
and every day I trace them with my tongue,
relishing their smoothness. And when I spit into the sink
and turn on the faucet, all that roughness
goes spiraling down the drain, through the pipes,
into that long, tentacled river flowing continuously
beneath our feet, carrying away all that we do not want
to think about or see again,
uniting stream with stream of effluent from my kitchen,
my bathroom, the neighbor's kitchen and bathroom,
every kitchen and bathroom in my small town,
in the neighboring city, in a thousand cities
across a continent.

Away it all goes but leaves behind trace after trace
in the pipes-become-channels-become-
subways that men can walk within and do
walk within, looking for the leaks and the corrosion
and the clogs that would flood a city street
or back up into your basement if there were not
someone   willing   to disappear
into the street's round, dark openings,
to descend into a chamber knee-deep

with the excrement and the sluice that we've all
tried to forget, that we all have forgotten
as soon as it leaves our sink or bathtub, and Mike Rowe
has made a television series, an entire career
out of the work that such men do (and such women),
unclogging the sewers, digging a river's worth of silt
from inside the dam, shovelful by shovelful,
stripping the feathers from bird carcasses,
carrying away the excrement of enormous animals,
because hard work
                      is beautiful

no matter the muck that you do it in,
and the men and women who do it are, yes,
                              beautiful,
the women with fingers raw from turning seams in the coat factory,
the men with faces blackened by the forge's fire,
the husband and wife toiling, bent over the long rows of strawberries,
their infant bundled under a tree at the field's edge, their ears listening
for the sound of approaching sirens.

In the Open

Yellow flower of spring. The whorled petals open.
Fragments of April sun. Why will this heart not open?

Don't stand there studying the porch rail's splinters.
Come in—the door is open.

How long will your red-rimmed eyes
turn toward him? This window will not open.

She faces the unfolding hours: a tangle of broken necklaces,
a crowd she shakes her fist at, a jar she cannot open.

The lock is turned, the bars are drawn, the proprietor
has left the building. When will this star-crossed café reopen?

She's dusting their last conversation for prints, logging each smile
and grimace, processing the physical evidence. This case remains open.

What I did That Day

Watched you pack your bags,
back the rusty pickup out of the driveway.

What comes back to me: the gray sheen of the harbor,
the white pelican's bright, indifferent eye.

Again the killdeer nest among the garden stones.
All afternoon, the neighbors are admonished.

A warm day in August, a moment of stillness.
Now begins the plunge toward autumn.

Warning: late in the evening, a startled newborn's wail.
The voice of your replacement.

The Knife

Gently it presses
sweet oil into crumb,
soft brie onto wafer.

Lightly it dices,
dances through carrot,
onion and garlic.

In swift movement, cleaves
the glistening orange,
provokes the glad thwack

of melon, sundered.
Divides flank from loin
from rib from brisket.

In the bright theater,
pierces sleeping flesh,
exposes tendon,

ligament, bursa.
Excises gray
glistening tumor:

Death carried away
in a silver bowl.

Standing Upright

I will admit, I was a sucker for those broad shoulders.
My knees went weak, I fell for a Norse god's shoulders.

The camera catches them in some far field. We gaze.
She sees only the row she plows, the gun he shoulders.

Who could believe the crime, the fall, the long disgrace?
They trusted in his *upright as the word of God* shoulders.

We saw a twisted spine, a shuffling step.   He
felt music spin his feet beneath those odd shoulders.

At dusk he hears the spirits' ragged voices;
dreads the beast's hot breath/paw at his shoulder.

She hisses at the new day's offerings,
phantoms lifting from the rosy dawn's shoulders.

The poet's forty days crossing the desert
have yielded fragments—pelvis, femur, jaw, shoulder.

Fleeing Nebraska

They set out for New York, but life
bitch-slapped them back to Omaha.

That's all she had to say about it.

Transcontinental

I am a
series of spaces.
Fill and
empty. Fill
and empty.

An iron gash
across the cheek
of this town. A
missile sent out
from the city.
Catastrophe bearing down
on the bedroom
at midnight.

I pass by without
slowing.
I never leave.

Without opening my mouth,
I will wail. I will

wail.

Dead Metaphors

This city built unto ourselves,
granite and marble edifices
side by side, the narrow lanes,
columns and pediments,
the grand avenues.

These specimens in rows,
ranked and labeled,
the closed cabinet,
the etched and jeweled cases.

This fleet, these brave vessels
without a flag, without a port,
rudderless, never listing
or coming about, riding quietly
a dark and featureless sea.

Institutional Memory

The police called at the house
late one night. They asked for Mother.
"Charlie Winston walked.
You'll call the judge?" Three in the morning

she was at that wooden desk, wood black
from years of smoke-
filled meetings, nurses and shrinks puffing
smoke, trying to hold together a house

of charred black souls that tried to fall apart.
But Mother rose at six and went there every morning,
smiled and said hello to moon-faced Louie
who walked in endless, arcing circles, slowly

walked inside the fence until a path was worn
into the smoke-gray dirt. The dour red buildings
emptied every morning just after breakfast, bodies
from their houses spilling onto lush green lawns.

At ten Mother would walk down the endless
hallways, over miles of black flecks in beige linoleum.
She would see a black-soled shoe sail out of a doorway,
hear the brisk walk of Margaret, who soothes, plays the mother,

wafts imagined smoke from Marvin's eyes;
would hear shrieks that carried almost to our house
where I woke every morning to oatmeal
and the smell of coffee. Father with his morning paper

would slip scraps of bacon to our Labrador. The black
trunks of oak trees disappeared above the house,
and I watched nuthatches that walked
down their sides, little birds with too-large

heads the color of smoke. Once in a while, my mother
would take me with her. I sat at my mother's
desk for hours in the morning, filling little slots
with paper clips and rubber bands. Cigarette smoke

drifted from the hall, where teenagers sat
in black vinyl chairs watching game shows.
If one of them walked toward me
I closed the door and thought of my house:

of Mother sitting in our lovely white house
that smelled like coffee every morning;
of black tree trunks and soulful birds that walk
upside-down with feathers the color of smoke.

Embrace

In the dream, I slip out of my skin.
Below the knee, it slides off
like a boot. And then the thighs,
like delicate sheets of paper unrolling.
And upward until I stand,
tender and quivering, muscle
and tendon and vessel, articulated bone
in the cool air of evening.
The rain begins and I
feel it then—

Landscape with Trees

after a collage by Thomas Terceira, "Metamorphosis #2"

The birds
              gaze without
alarm or
   disappointment
without one second of
regret but we

look back
        look
over our
   shoulder
over

a landscape littered
with routes
            not
taken with
white petals
with
wings that will
  not
            lift us

Updraft

A Golden Shovel on C.K. Williams's "Danger"

No matter how carefully you watch
~~your tongue~~ your language, the blue light will out
you.
Dissemble with all your might.
Feint, juke, take flight, feel yourself fall-
ing. The words you speak drop, heavy. Dark. As
morning dawns, answers collect. Disembody *that*.
And how the papery spirits rise. And how the mountain fell.

You are a teenage girl

without a Kotex.
Even without the mirror,
you see the darkness
spreading. The hallway holds
a thousand pairs of eyes.
The final bell will never ring.
Your body will complete
its humiliation, limp hair,
bloom of acne, cloud
of odors.

You are a man
who doesn't remember his name.
You wake each day
in an unfamiliar room.
You remember home, but no one
will take you there.
Your shirt buttons
have rearranged themselves.
Someone takes your hand and
leads you where you do not want
to go.

You are the mother of God
without a husband.
You walk the alleys at night
listening for the angel's voice.
You will wrap him in swaddling clothes
and leave him on bent cardboard
beneath the yellow light
for a stranger to find
in the morning.

You are a teenage boy
without a gun.
The world
bares its black teeth
at you.
You feel the itch, hear

the staccato,
see the twisted faces,
the bodies falling, glorious
ribbons of red
across the black linoleum.

Raising the Temperature

Maybe what I need is a hot little number,
cherry red with bucket seats
and four on the floor, something that can
roll out hot from the gate,
tires smoking, leaving a hot
trail for everyone else to follow.

Maybe what I need is some hot tubbing,
some steam rising around my ears,
some bubbles leaving me all hot headed,
your fingers tracing lines down my
hot pink thigh.

Maybe I just need some hot words,
some passion making its way down the page,
lines dripping desire and swirling
with the wanton abandon of a
steaming summer afternoon.

III
The Earth's Skin

Spinning the Stone

Late evening snow spooning the earth,
caress of twig and branch, her lover the earth.

You pour, golden liqueur, through my fingers.
Where shall I seek you? Over the earth.

Children flicker, the long street's narrow shadows.
Shattering of stones; vanishes the earth.

Valley floor subsides, distends.
Black mountain shudders, ragged husk of earth.

In December darkness I wonder,
From what ear depends the blue jewel of earth?

Earth's Bones

i.
The children beside the river finger pebbled gabbro,
caress blood-red jasper and hematite,
tongue quartz's milky smoothness.
One hundred stones: the earth carried in each pocket.

ii.
The bulldozer rakes the hillside, leaves a trail
of newborn schist and granite.

iii.
The trees wrap their roots around pillows of stone.
The fish take cold shelter in the shadow of stones.
Our meal before us, we do not think of stones.

iv.
The tree awaits
the lichen's bitter work
upon the stone.

v.
They have stood five thousand years.
They send their silent voices, still,
toward the long-empty chambers of our gods.
Place your hand on this worn edge
shaped, once, by my blows.
Gazing across this emptiness,
you will not find our bones.

vi.
I gaze across last summer's clean-picked soil:
the earth grins at me with its teeth of stone.

Forty-seven Miles above Lock Number 1

1965

I'm four years old. My uncle and I
stand, parka-wrapped, on solid ground.
Ten feet away, the rain-swollen Mississippi
laps the threshold of a neighbor's mobile home.
She stands in the doorway, reaches inside
for a cardboard box and hands it
out the door to her husband, knee-deep in icy water.
He tosses box after box into the bed of his tan pickup truck.
A twenty-foot slab of ice sails
between elm trees. The woman leaps
from her front step to dry ground.
Her home sways, then floats toward the channel,
as deliberate and graceful as the geese
lounging on the far side of the river.
When it's gone, I imagine it bobbing, tilting,
cut free by spring thaw.
"Where will it go?" I ask my uncle.
"All the way." he answers. "To the Gulf of Mexico."

1968

"Always stay three feet from the edge."
My father's finger traces a line in the grass.
"Why?" I wonder. I look at that
three feet—solid earth, it seems to me,
before lawn ceases and the earth
cascades in showers of loam, sand, and gneiss
to the edge of the Mississippi.
"Because it might give way and drop you fifteen feet."
I shudder and marvel at nature's
compliance: three feet and no more the river
may undermine. The rest is ours. I look
over my shoulder and see the long, white wall,
the back side of our three-bedroom rambler.

1981

"You can't swim upstream," I tell my boyfriend.
We stand at water's edge, the riverbank towering
behind us, and watch the river's stillness until
a twig spins by, traveling faster than a man can walk.
Water purls over stones. One half
of an oak tree floats by, leaves shuddering.
We step in. Water tugs at our feet, ankles, calves.
By mid-thigh, we lean our full weight upstream,
dig our heels into gravel that deserts us, slips away
so that we inch downriver. Brad doesn't believe me.
He faces the current and launches himself,
his long, work-strengthened arms swinging the crawl.
He turns toward me with each breath,
and I watch the dark circle of his mouth, again and again,
as he floats by me, feet first, toward the Gulf of Mexico.

Stripes

          I saw
          a small
          snake
              coiled
                    at the edge
             of the sidewalk.
      His lovely
    stripes
twisted and
        returned
           upon them-
                selves.
                    I knelt,
            looked in his
        watching eye;
       he
                              slipped
      turned

disappeared

              beneath a grating.

    What
          other poems
                    would I find
              if I peered
          into the
    dark and
narrow spaces,
       holes and
           crevices,
                the refuges of the many
            distasteful
        beautiful
     crawling
       tunneling
         things?

The Poet Is Asked to Write about a Tree

Living in the city, I forgot
the look of an untended tree,
its roots clinging to
some half-eroded slope,
canted crown twisting toward
a ragged spot of sky.
I'd forgotten trunks
mortared and softened
with damp, pale lichen,
last decade's stormfall
slumped against a neighboring trunk.
How no one trims away
the shattered limb
nor tidies the forest floor of woody
corpses, bark loosening.
How, within an upturned ball of roots,
life gladly plants its foot on
pending death.

Paddling the Mississippi, South of St. Cloud

From the river's edge the green world
pushes up—basswood, oak,
box elder—glittering in summer heat.

I watch a cliff of loam slide by, its feet
a drift of agate, schist and granite.
On the river's other bank, a heron

lifts its heavy weight. The paddle in my hand
slices the river's muddy calm. Rising from the water,
the remnant of a bridge, a stump of stone.

A curtain parts to show a bit of pasture,
six Holsteins, six jaws tracing easy circles.
Paddle across my knees, I turn to see

an osprey at her nest, a bicycle's bent tire,
a haloed cottonwood, leaning, ready
to lift its feet and rest upon the river,

to relinquish the world, leaving behind
one small, melting wound.

Sunday Morning Samba

What do you suppose
a lizard does on Sunday mornings?
Does he sleep in, read the paper,
ask for extra bacon with his espresso?
Does his swivel eye
light on the latest TV ad?
Does his long tongue flick across
the kitchen table
to fondly swipe a beloved snout?

Or does he rise to his full height, toes splayed,
belly white against the picture window,
scandalizing the neighbors?

Perhaps he busies himself
tightening the loose doorknob,
unclogging the stubborn drain,
peering toward the refrigerator's petulant squeal.

I hope that he grabs the missus
from behind, and that the two of them
go dancing dirty across the hallway's
cool, smooth tile, their tails twitching
the unpremeditated meter
of a swivel-hipped samba. I hope,
before the afternoon company shows up,
they slip away, strip off the old skins,
and slowly twine, the two of them,
swimming once again toward that old double helix
of Sunday morning desire.

The cold of January

shines bright blue,
long-shadowed,
filamental.
I walk the
brittle, attenuated
sidewalk. I am nothing
but a black shard,
nothing but
the crisp report
of my footfalls,
rising
solitary
and disappearing
into the white
silent distances
between the
unfamiliar houses.

Hearing the News

January 19, 1873

It was twelve days
before we realized
before each one could hear
the same story from Arthur
and Bertie and William.
Three days for the storm to stop blowing
Another two to dig one's way
to the hog pen and the barn
to throw hay to the starving mare.
Another week before
the wagons could make their way to town
before folks could hear
who lived
who had died
who lay with frozen
blackened feet
waiting for the surgeon.

I felt the storm's chill again
as Mathias told the story
how after the search party returned home
he spotted John treading the path to the barn
wearing his favorite, the blue soldier overcoat,
his hands tucked up under the cape.
"'John Warner! We thought you were frozen to death!'
'I am,' came the reply, 'and you'll find my body
in the Brickman slough.'
Before I could answer, he had vanished."

I couldn't speak
that afternoon
sitting with John's widow,
my sister,
when she told me she'd been roused in the night
by a rap on the door
and a voice that called out,
"Do you know your husband's frozen to death?"

"Francis and I both flew to the door, but there was no one there, and no track in the snow."

First of June

This morning, summer rode its jake brakes
into town. We stood beside the road,
our hair blown back, our ears ringing

after the engine's roar, watching
paper sacks tossed in the wake,
winter's wilted remnants in the ditches.

Afternoon. Winter's survivors, all of us,
stand sun-dazzled, wide-eyed. The local boys
have hauled jet skis from garages

and tossed them into the water.
I watch the riders spin and rear and plunge,
their engines singing in scallops.

Just past the buoy, young men lounge in the gleaming boat
belonging to their father, showing their stomachs winter white.
On shore, the beach walkers mince among winterkill,

wide-stepping over sunfish skeleton, crappie's
dried and tunneled flesh. The wind strips sand from the beach
and hurls it against the backs of the walkers' knees.

I shield my eyes and gaze across water the color of glowing flint,
gashed by whitecaps that bloom and fade.
Summer's bright power pulses on my skin.

Two visits to paradise

I.

The beach slopes like an anvil to the sea.
I sit and read Fodor's. Those early playboys—
Rockefeller, Olds, all their ascotted rivals—
raced these hard, smooth miles beside salt water
in Fiats and Rolls Royces.

Everything here is hard, indeed—
the sand that bruises my heels, the glass-and-steel
hotels, insolent shards crowding the ocean,
the waves breaking and drumming
before their long run up the unyielding slope.

I wade into the surf until I feel
the tide's push and pull.
Diving, surfacing, I blow and spit.
So much salt! So much salt!
And leagues and
unending leagues of it.

II.

Green thorns of the palo verde
Ancient liturgical pose of the saguaro
Ocotillo's spiny exuberance
Desiccated seabed floor pierced through
with the peaks of buried mountains
Do those who come here recognize
the dwelling of an unfamiliar god

The Famous Anoka Potato

"The finest eating potato grown is the Minnesota potato."
—*The New York Times, September 25, 1903*

I wonder if he laid them here, old Reuel Hall,
these worn bricks, this remnant of a wall.
He knew better than to listen to those Boston bankers.
He knew to buy a ticket, to ride west across the Ohio
and north along the Mississippi. As the train rolled past Lake Pepin,
he already saw the belts flying and the drive shafts turning,
the maw of the grater devouring the clean-washed russets,
the wagons laboring toward St. Paul, carrying the pure, shining starch
to kitchens and laundries across a young continent.

He knew potato country when he saw it—the sandy soil
where plump tubers would burst from the earth, ready
for the bins, for the troughs and the washers, ready
to form that pulpy slurry, the snowy granules in the rivers of water.
The vines sent up their purple flowers. The farmers filled their carts.
Wives on Saturday left spacious kitchens to come to town,
to spend their potato money on gingham and glass and sweet
molasses. The talk at the local tavern was all the potato. The city
council kept its eye on the potato. The mayor watched the laborers
with their shovels and their wheelbarrows, smoothing the new road
to carry the potato. When twenty years had passed, they gathered,
every one, to toast old Reuel Hall, who sat before them, smiling that
gracious, distant smile. They knew to put their trust in the potato.

Old Reuel Hall rests, this day, beneath a distant stone. The corn
stands tall, the beans hang heavy, here, above the sandy soil.
A starchy redolence has settled from the air. The Pearson boys
cast their eyes down rows of corn, calculating bushels and futures.
Their father stands here, too, and remembers his father,
driving down the long, straight rows on the old Allis-Chalmers.
They look across this field and do not see, not one of them,
the purple flowers nodding in the early June sun.

January Morning, Lake Superior, Rocky Beach

A man, a child, and a dog
walk toward the water.
The man wears a blue coat.
The child wears a yellow hat.
The man picks the child up
and sets the child down.
Boulders—polished, ice-sheathed—
cluster beside the water.
The dog pulls at the leash.
The water stretches, a glistening sheet,
toward the low sun. The child
reaches the tip of a mitten
toward the frozen ground.
Beside the man, a stream
empties itself into the lake,
water rushing beneath ledges of ice.
The man picks the child up
and sets the child down.
The child points.
The dog turns this way and that.
Transparent ice trembles at the rim.
Sunlight shines through shreds of fog.
The child crosses the beach. He
hoists a pillow of rock, carries it
to the man and sets it down.
Around a glistening knoll, water
contracts and recedes like a heartbeat.
The man picks the child up
and sets the child down.

Beside the Kennedy Expressway

The earth's skin pulls tight in places,
scales and thickens,
throbs mottled red and white.

Near Thirteenth Street today,
I noticed the sidewalks
filling with pale, blonde young men.

Have you noticed
how water pours from the edges of a city?
Beneath the Sears Tower,
the earth is chalk-dry and brittle.

My brother scaled an office building once.
From the twenty-second story, he said,
the people looked like beads
scattering
on a polished linoleum floor.

The edges
crack, turn to gray
and soften in the summer sun.

Terror wore us

like a pencil skirt, whispered
burnt flesh, failed trajectories,
the desiccating emptiness between the stars.
In the living room, the air grew thin.
Translunar darkness
seeped between the ceiling tiles.

    Cigarette smoke. Gin and tonics.

We lurched as our planet shook,
as we watched husbands
climb into the great beast,
let it fling them into blackness.
We held our breath through lunar silence,

    The cameras. Our clenched fists.

through re-entry's conflagration.
Our children leapt through earth days but we
felt the weight of galaxies, sustained ourselves
with games of bridge and Diazepam.
We had strapped ourselves in for this journey but,

    Pitch, roll, yaw.

more than once,
we prayed for separation burn,
for a ship to carry us back to
ordinary, earth-bound lives.

    Abigail Trafford: "As the men got set to fly to the
    moon, we Apollo families built a capsule of our own."

Acknowledgments

I am grateful, first of all, to Brad Bouma, who may not entirely understand my obsession with poetry, but who has never complained about the hours I devote to it. I'm grateful to Susan Chambers, whose efforts in creating and sustaining various poet communities enabled my poet self to blossom. A profound thank you to Nichole Borg for her focused and helpful feedback on this manuscript. I'm grateful to all of the poets in the League of Minnesota Poet and its chapters for the joy of sharing a life of poetry with so many supportive souls.

I also gratefully acknowledge the following journals and anthologies, where a number of these poems first appeared:

2River View: "Swimming Dock, Longville, Minnesota" and "The Body Remembers"

Agates: "Song of the Seventh Day"

County Lines: 87 Minnesota Counties, 130 Minnesota Poets: "The Famous Anoka Potato"

Main Channel Voices: "The Knife"

McNeese Review: "In Which He Tries to Make Me Understand"

What Light poetry series at mnartists.org: "Hearing the News"

Natural Bridge: "Color Shift"

Rattle: "The Things We Forget"

Rock & Sling: "Solid Things"

San Pedro River Review: "First of June"

Talking Stick: "Afternoon Call" and "Sunday Morning Samba"

Jana Bouma's poems have appeared in journals and anthologies including Rattle, *The McNeese Review, Natural Bridge, The 2River View,* and *San Pedro River Review,* and as a text in David Kassler's *Choral Song Cycle on Texts of Minnesota Poets.* The recipient of a Prairie Lakes Regional Arts Council Emerging Artist Grant, she earned her PhD in English Literature from the University of Nebraska-Lincoln. She has worked as a mechanical engineer, a college English instructor and a freelance writer. She lives with her husband in southern Minnesota where she works as a college advisor for first-generation college students.

www.ingramcontent.com/pod-product-compliance
Lightning Source LLC
Chambersburg PA
CBHW030058170426
43197CB00010B/1579